Destiny Shaker

Destiny Shaker

**Destiny has an Appointment and
Prayer Keeps it on Schedule**

Carla Gaskins

Cover Layout: JWGraphics

To order additional copies of this book, contact:

ONE DOMINION PUBLISHING

a subsidiary of
Revolutionary Disciples Media
PO Box 1481
Hiram, GA 30141
www.revolutionarydisciples.com

Book ID:

DEDICATION

This book is dedicated to my three Grandmothers, who were the first intercessors that introduced me to prayer: Rebecca Shepherd, Alice Dailey, and Henrietta Bates.

ACKNOWLEDGEMENTS

To Dr. Glenda Sherman and Apostle Regina Martin, for all your prophetic impartation and your contribution to my growth in ministry.

I also want to acknowledge my Pastor, my spiritual father, Pastor Vincent Campbell, of The Faith Center in Tucker, Georgia for allowing me to carry the ministry in prayer.

FORWARD

I have watched Minister Carla Gaskins ministry from afar and I love what God is doing through her. She has such a great passion for prayer and intercession so writing this forward was easy. Destiny Shaker is a must have for this season, it prepares the reader to shift into a greater place of intercession and insight. Min Carla Gaskins has a way of breaking things down that make it simple for the reader to understand. God has given her a unique anointing to articulate spiritual matters, she is a gift to the body of Christ. I recently invited her to our Forerunners Women and Girls summit, and I was truly blessed with the information and the knowledge that she poured into us on that day. I believe that Destiny Shaker will truly bless many. In a time where many things are being defined as non-essential, this book is an essential to your library of books.

Dr. Regina Martin
Embassy Church of South Florida

TABLE OF CONTENTS

INTRODUCTION

To the Christian, prayer is vital, it is a necessity, it is oxygen to our spirit. When we pray, we are connecting our spirit to God's Spirit. Prayer moves us from a state of hopelessness to a river of hope. To the Christian it is not just something we do, but it is the air we breathe.

Many people do not think about prayer until they find themselves in front of the red sea with walls of mountains on each side and the Egyptians behind them, then suddenly they cry out to God in desperation. But when you discover the power of prayer and intercession you will never be the same again.

As destiny shakers, in our spirit there is a cry for more, "deep calling unto deep" Psalm 42:7, because of this cry we have been shaken and awaken to tap into the prophetic voice of God through prayer and intercession. This call of God is about a personal and deep encounter with the Father. It is about the altar of the cross through his Son Jesus who died for us. And this book reminds us that it all starts at the altar.

This book will help you to discover not only the powerful principals of prayer, but the power of prayer that brings you into a closer and deeper relationship with the Father each time you pray. Each chapter is filled with the rich treasures of faith and trials of life and ministry.

This book captivates your heart and mind in a way that makes you feel like you are hearing directly from the throne of God - who's talking to you about prayer and what prayer actually means to Him, and why prayer is not to be taken so lightly.

This book is birthed from the heart of a true prayer warrior and intercessor who has gone through many trials and experiences in life which validates her to author this book.

Be blessed!

Dr. Glenda Sherman

Appointed for Such A Time as This –
www.glendashermanministries.org

CHAPTER ONE

<u>Why People Do Not Pray</u>

...and prayerlessness is called a sin.
1Thessalonians 5:17

The average Christian spends less than ten minutes each day in prayer. One of many reasons people do not pray is they do not believe. We believe in everything else but prayer. I am amazed at how many can give 40-plus hours to a company and have more faith in it to pay them than to believe the God they serve to answer prayers. Many do not believe God hears their prayers, or is able to answer our prayer, or request is too big for Him, He cannot handle it, or He is too far removed. God cares enough to intervene if we just believe. If you do not believe or have confidence, then maybe that is why He has not answered.

...if you have faith the size of a mustard seed.
Luke 17:6

Unbelief has your answers to prayer locked up in the realm of the spirit. We live in a time where miracles, signs, and wonders are not being taught. We are not teaching the word, regarding faith anymore. We Have been told that we can just name it and claim it. Great motivational speeches are given in church, with little to no Word of God given to back up what is being said. We also live in a right now society. No one wants to wait anymore; no one wants to sacrifice anymore. Do we have to jump through hoops for God to answer prayers? No, we do not, however there is a process in going to God in prayer and it starts with faith. A lack of faith is why people are not praying. Lack of trust in God is why people do not pray.

> *how, then, can they call on the one they have not*
> *believed in? And how can they believe in the*
> *one of whom they have not heard? And how can*
> *they hear without someone preaching to them?*
> Romans 10:14-17

Our relationship with God is important and believing and trusting him is vital to your prayer life. I do not care what you think is too big for God, it is still small in His eyes and you can believe it is nothing new to him. He has done it before. I remember when God moved in a way in my life when I had to believe Him for something big. I had a desire to be a mother; trying for years to get pregnant. I prayed to God because I believed He could do it. But let me tell you first it was not immediate. It was 19 years of waiting on God to answer. My faith was tested in the process and it was not easy.

Another reason people do not pray is the lack of patience. Do you know patience is connected to trust, hope, faith, love, and good character? Romans 12:12 says, *let your hope keep you joyful, be patient in troubles, and pray at all times.* I can tell you in the 19 years I waited I developed character, joy, and patience. If you want to be someone's mother, you need that and more. He was making me ready. In the meantime, I became a mother to three children my husband at the time had before we married.

Instantly I became a full-time mom to two of them. They were part of my process. I watched so many friends and family get pregnant and have babies. Even my nieces grew up and had babies before me. I celebrated every single one of them. I went to baby showers, playing games and even became godmother to my best friend's son. I gave into what I wanted for myself. Was it easy? No, but I knew the promises of God that were given to me would manifest. In April of 2003, my husband and I received a prophecy that I would have a baby. Five prophets surrounded and prayed over us. I was overwhelmed because my silent prayers were going to be answered after so many years of waiting. It was two months later I learned I was pregnant.

Then November 13th, 2003 the unthinkable happened. I lost my baby. I could not believe what my doctor said at the regular doctor's appointment. Her words rang loudly, and my entire heart sank when she said, "There is no heartbeat!" I was sent to a neonatal specialist for another opinion. My doctor was a Believer and she did not want to believe what she saw on the ultrasound. She prayed with me before I left to go over to the specialist. It was confirmed that day my baby was gone. Just like that. To make matters worse, I had to schedule an induction to give birth to my now-deceased baby. It was the longest four days of my life.

I felt like someone snatched something from me that left a void no one could fill. I cried for weeks, so much I had to take pills to sleep, just so I was not crying all the time. My husband did not know what to do or say. I remember one late night at around 12 a.m. he was watching a Ministry on the word network. I was awakened by a powerful prayer. I sat straight up in the bed speaking in my heavenly language. Who in the world was this person praying so powerfully to the point of pulling me out of my sleep? Prophetess Angie Ray, she has since gone home to be with the Lord. It was the prayer that came into my home through a TV screen that rescued me out of grief and despair.

I was reminded that my prayer life allowed me to get pregnant when I had been told so many times before the loss of my baby, I would never get pregnant. Just because I lost my baby did not mean God did not keep His promise. I told God in Worship at church laid out on the altar with a dead baby in my womb that if He never gave me another baby, I still trust Him and believe in Him.

If He did it once He could do it again. I promised to love the two He already gave me. I had my Hannah moment. A year later April 2004, Easter Sunday, on the altar at church God spoke to me and said cover and pray for your baby. I did and the only person heard my prayer was my aunt who was right next to me at the altar. I had not even taken a pregnancy test. The day after I took one it read positive and January 2005, I had a healthy beautiful baby girl. It was my hope, faith and trust in God that carried me 19 years.

We must develop our faith—we cannot live in the same faith for everything! It must grow and stretch for the small and the Impossible. Faith works, so work your faith. We must not be lazy in prayer. Hebrews 6:12 states, *we do not want you to become lazy, but to imitate those who through faith and patience inherit what has been promised.*

Laziness is another reason people do not pray. There is no room and no answers for the lazy Christian. The MIND must be transformed by the renewing of the Mind. A lazy Christian lacks Integrity and is undisciplined in prayer and bible study. This may be the reason many do not see prayer as a way for God to move on their behalf.

How can you believe in God when you do not take the time to know Him or allow Him to develop you in a lifestyle of Prayer? People do not prioritize prayer. Other things take priority over prayer. Chasing careers, securing the bag, or a combination of social media. Even people in full-time Ministry let things sneak up on them and rob God of quality time and prayer. Sermon preparations, visitations, Church administration, counseling Etc., nothing should take time away from God. Martin Luther "said I have so much to do that I shall have to spend the first three hours in prayer."

We have become discouraged. Losing my baby could have discouraged me. But it did not. Prayer revived me and reminded me how I was able to get pregnant in the first place. Whenever disappointment comes it should not discourage us when we have a history in prayer with God. I know God answered at least one prayer in your life even if all you said was Jesus from a near car accident and you survived it. In Luke 18:1-8, the woman was persistent with the judge. She never gave up when he ignored her, refused to listen to her. He gave in to her because she never gave up on hearing her case. God bears long with you and that is enough to encourage you not to be discouraged. Continue seeking God until you see results; ask God for a Holy Spirit of prayer.

The Spirit you received does not make you slaves, so that you live in fear again; rather, the Spirit you received brought about your adoption to sonship. And by him we cry, "Abba, Father."
Romans 8:15

CHAPTER TWO

<u>First Things First: Repent</u>

And in seeing repent
for the kingdom of God is at hand!
Matthew 3:2

Why is repenting important? It frees you from the sin that
holds you captive and turns you away from the road that
leads to guilt and deceit. It is necessary to repent before
you go before God. It puts you in position to gain access
to the ear and heart of God. Let us explore some things
that will help you understand why we must repent. When
we live a sinful life, we can miss God and His hand in
our lives.

In Matthew 3:2, it says *repent, for the kingdom of God is
at hand*. Meaning salvation and all that God has for us
has come. For us to have access to the kingdom, we must
first repent. Repenting comes with benefits, such as
being free from the sin itself, guilt, condemnation
spiritual death and even natural death. We cannot go
through life without a spirit of conviction as a Believer.
Even non-believers have a moment of conviction, before
repenting and confessing Jesus as Lord. Conviction
brings about a repentant heart. Repenting is a spiritual
cleanse we need every day. Even before we pray, we
should have a moment of repentance. I noticed
something different with my time in prayer when I
sincerely repented first.

Let us look at Five Points of Repenting, that **I learned 2
decades ago** and how it shifts your prayer experience
with God...

1. Be honest about your need for repentance.

> *Blessed is the one whose sin the Lord does not count against them and in whose spirit is no deceit.* Psalm 32:2 NIV

This verse is a wonderful place to explore the nature and process of deep repentance, which requires honesty. No one comes to God with true repentance in their heart unless they first acknowledge their need for forgiveness and reconciliation with Him! Only those who have ceased trying to cover up their sin with self-righteousness and deceit can experience the deep and lasting change that comes only through repentance.

Let me share a time I had a moment of deep repentance. I remember after a divorce, I was angry, lonely, frustrated, and reckless; however, I was not fully aware of any of those emotions. I decided that I would take time out to hear from God for my life and just allowed this to be a time of healing and evaluation. Well, you know satan is <u>always</u> somewhere watching and waiting. He already knows your vices better than you. Well, my vices had always been men and seeking love anyway I could get it.

I remember a three-day span that changed my life. The devil brought three men I dated years prior to these three days into my life. The crazy thing was I had not seen any of them in over 20 plus years. They were old boyfriends from high school and after. They all were men that I loved in the past. Let me tell you the devil set me up good. Keep in mind, I am still talking about honest and deep repentance.

At the time, one of my friends had been asking me to go to church with her. A guy we grew up with was now a pastor. I kept telling her no, maybe another Sunday. So, lets revisit the event I mentioned, where I had sex with three different men over three days. Yes, you read that correctly, I had sex with three different men in three days…Thursday, Friday, and Saturday. Do not judge me! On that third day I felt ashamed and dirty, simply filthy. However, my Spirit was vexed, and I felt a tugging on me to ask for forgiveness.

You see I was already saved at the time. I was sold out for God or so I thought. Yet, I fell for the Temptation satan set before me. Late that Saturday night, my girlfriend called me and said, "I'm going to church in the morning, do you want to come with me?" I said, "yes," before she could finish. I was not sure if I were going so I could feel better or just scared God would kill me in my sleep if I said no—knowing what I did the previous three days. I just knew I needed that guilt assuaged. What better way to rid myself from it but by going to church?

Well Sunday morning came, and I was still alive! God did not kill me in my sleep. You must love God for how he gives us time to get it right? So off to church I went. Already feeling guilt for my actions and the thought of walking into church feeling like I had failed was more than I could bear. Every song pulled on my heart and the corporate prayer call was convicting me. By the time the word was delivered, I already had my mind made up to be honest with God, repent and rededicate my life.

Well before that could happen, the prophet called me from the back, to the front of the church, basically recounting the last three days of my life. God did <u>not</u> expose me, but he spoke enough through the man of God.

He also reiterated that he is a forgiving God and I knew then how much God loved me, even in my sinful ways. There on the floor crying my heart out, I repented for everything I had done up to that moment.

There in my honest and transparent moment with God, I did not care who heard or knew me. I acknowledged my sin and the need to repent. That changed my life forever and I never backslid. There was a deep, lasting change.

2. Acknowledge the danger of sin and the damage of guilt.

> *3. When I kept silent, my bones wasted away through my groaning all day long. 4 For day and night your hand was heavy on me; my strength was sapped as in the heat of summer.*
> Psalm 32: 3-4

Let us face it, we seek repentance because God's Holy Spirit convicts us. It is easy to blame others for our wrong, moodiness, and stress but the truth is, we feel bad because we have done wrong. David in these two verses describes physical and emotional symptoms associated with a guilty conscience. We must honestly assess the consequences of our sins, which means assessing personal consequences and the impact it has had and will continue to have on others! When I had sex with those three individuals, it was not just me, but the men partook also. Did I mention they were all married? Had I continued with them and not repented I was disrupting the lives of many. We must understand that the importance of repenting is for you, but the damage cannot be measured. I thank God for mercy.

3. Another part of repenting is your confession.

Then I acknowledged my sin to you and did not cover up my iniquity. I said, "I will confess my transgressions to the Lord." Psalm 32: 5a

David never failed to confess his wrongs. I believe God loved David for many reasons and one of them was his honesty when he was wrong; even as King, he was not above repenting. He knew when he was wrong

When I was on the floor of that church, it did not matter to me who heard my confession to God while repenting. It was between me and God. He is the only one who can forgive you of your sins, not man or woman. Truth be told, the people you are worried about need to repent themselves! We all do every day to be honest. Deep repentance demands full confession. Seems like common sense, the only way to truly be covered by Christ is to fully expose yourself. During the process of repenting, we must fight to be completely transparent before God and about the deepness of our sin. Only brutal honesty will lead to freedom and joy.

4. Hide in God,

5 Then I acknowledged my sin to you and did not cover up my iniquity. said, "I will confess my transgressions to the Lord." And you forgave the guilt of my sin. 6 Therefore let all the faithful pray to you while you may be found; surely the rising of the mighty waters will not reach them. 7 You are my hiding place; you will protect me from trouble and surround me with songs of deliverance. Psalm 32: 5b-7

Why do we need to hide in God? It is our protection from sin, and it positions us for access in prayer. When we hide behind things that are not of God, He cannot see us. Repentance is a big part of prayer and being able to commune with God. Hiding in anything or any place outside of God is an indication you need to repent. *When we hide in Him, we will not have the need to hide behind religion or the image we created to maintain the wrong we WANT to do.* Adam and Eve hid behind the leaves they covered themselves with from God. They hid behind creation from the Creator! They were ashamed and masked their sins.

Self-made righteousness is not the place to hide to make us appear more acceptable. We are not fooling God and certainly not fooling ourselves. The true mark of change and the true mark of repentance is when you hide in God alone. It is not enough just to repent of open sins, but also for your attempt to cover the sin. Stop hiding in your effort to cover your sins and hide in God.

5. Seize the hope.

> *Many are the woes of the wicked, but the Lord's unfailing love surrounds the one who trusts in him.* Psalm 32: 10

How can we be sure God will forgive us? We can be assured of His unfailing love. We have documented examples and promises throughout history of what he has done and daily reminders in our lives of how he shows love towards us. These are the promises fulfilled by Jesus. He promised Adam and Eve would crush the enemy. He promised Abraham would claim and protect the people. He promised Moses He would provide a way for sinful humans to be able to relate to a Holy God. He promised David an eternal King for his people. From the beginning of time up to this very moment we must desire and seek repentance. God has been saying and continues to say, I love you. I will not leave you. I Am enough.

CHAPTER THREE

Types of Intercessors

Priestly Intercessor

I want to share some revelations with you on an interesting topic, about four types of intercessors in today's world. There are a lot of things going on; a lot of conference calls and advertisements are emerging. Intercessors and prophetic intercessors are being called out, but many times we have rarely been given the definition for these experiences and they are nothing like the spirit that we have been flowing in. So, I want to give you some nomenclature, some definitions, and some articulation for spiritual occurrences that are happening within our local churches, especially when it relates to prayer intercession and it is not one size fits all. Every intercessor is different. Each has a different anointing, different mantle, different wisdom, and a different metron. Just like the United States of America's military. There is an Army, Air Force, Navy, the Marines, National Guard and Coast Guard. Each one of them have a different assignment.

It is the same way with intercessors. We all have a unique assignment to ensure that all the bases are covered in the realm of the spirit. I want to begin by sharing the scripture and this is in, 1st Timothy 2:1, *I exhort therefore, that, first of all, supplications, prayers, intercessions, and giving of thanks, be made for all men.* The Bible says prayers, intercession, and supplications, which is plural. That means that there are numerous types of prayers and numerous types of intercessors. I am going to explain it and dive into it a little.

Let us get into the first type of intercessor. The first type of intercessor is called the Priestly intercessor, the generals. They plead the cases of others before the Throne of Heaven in prayer. According to Hebrews 4:16, we must approach God's throne of grace with confidence; so that we may receive mercy and find Grace to help us in our time of need. Intercessors are so powerful because they are like lawyers. If you ever have to go before a judge or before the Throne, you hire a lawyer, who is then assigned to negotiate on your behalf and to present your case before the Throne, so that perhaps the judge will favor you. It is the same way with intercessors. When we go before the throne of grace, we are like lawyers in a court room. Pleading the cases of earth, so heaven can intervene in the affairs of man in our times of need, and so that heaven can begin to rule in our favor.

When I think about it, whenever Heaven rules on a case in Heaven, the Earth must submit to heaven and its decree. If you can win in the court of Heaven, all the courts of Earth must line up with what heaven has decreed. That is why prayer is so important. Intercessors are important, whether you need God to give you favor in a legal situation, you need a promotion, or you need favor in any type of situation. It is very important for us to have these intercessors go before God on our behalf. A perfect example is when my sister was facing 30 years in prison for something she did not do, I went on a 40-day fast and prayed for her. I literally saw during my time of prayer what was going on in the courtroom. I could see the district attorney and the defense attorney representing her before the judge and everything that I saw in the spirit, my mother called me later in the day and explained to me what happened in that courtroom. I saw it exactly as it happened. Praise God, my sister served no time because I went before the throne of grace on her behalf and warred on her behalf as a Priestly intercessor. What an awesome privilege to go before the throne of grace.

Prayer Warrior

The next intercessor is called the Prayer Warrior. These types of intercessors are the ones who are assigned to receive warfare strategies and tactics. They then implement them, to overthrow powers of darkness and to release breakthroughs. These intercessors have a militant spirit and are skilled in the art of spiritual warfare. Eph 6:12 says, *for our struggle is not against flesh and blood, but against the rulers, against the authorities, against the powers of this dark world and against the spiritual forces of evil in the heavenly realms.* Every day the powers of Darkness are working against us to take us out. Every day we are in warfare. Every day the powers of Darkness are working against us. Therefore, prayer warriors are important because they are the military strategists of the Kingdom of Heaven. They can receive downloads of how to win and overcome in battles and go into the realm of the spirit and fight evil spirits and forces.

They can <u>block</u> things. They are very powerful intercessors. Eph 6:18 tells us to *pray always with all prayer and supplication in the Spirit and watching thereunto with all perseverance and supplication for all saints.* Prayer warriors win breakthroughs for us in many different areas in which we are attacked, whether it is in our family, finances, or relationships. *War Room* is a great example of how a prayer warrior breaks through. The older woman teaches the young wife how to win the war against her marriage and family. Prayers of the righteous are the greatest military force in the heavens and on earth.

Prophetic Intercessor

This intercessor is assigned to discern heavens sonogram, to birth the will, purpose, and plan of God in earth. Through travailing, they carry the burden of the Lord and pray only what they hear heaven speaking.

> *But if they be prophets, and if the word of the Lord be with them, let them now make intercession to the Lord of hosts, that the vessels which are left in the house of the Lord, and in the house of the king of Judah, and at Jerusalem, go not to Babylon.* Jeremiah 27:18

Heaven is pregnant with so much. God wants to release His promises in the earth realm. He places it in the womb of the prophetic intercessor. And in their intercession, they can cause the heavens to contract. So, whatever is in the unseen that is incubating in the realm of the spirit, whether it is over our churches or families, they can push it out from the spirit realm. From the unseen to the seen realm, prophetic intercessors are very powerful as well.

Anna knew that the son of God was to be born. She labored in the temple with prayer and fasting. She was birthing the son of God in the earth! Even Jesus had to be birthed through in the spirit. Prayer is the conduit for the purposes and plans of God in the earth realm.

*And she was a widow of about fourscore and
four years, which departed not from the temple,
but served God with fastings and prayers night
and day.* Luke 2:37

Watchman Intercessor

These intercessors build hedges and walls to protect.
They protect individual regions and Nations. The word
Watchman in the original Hebrew comes from the word
Shemar which means to guard, to protect, to encircle, and
to build a hedge.

> *6 I have set watchmen upon thy walls, O
> Jerusalem, which shall never hold their peace
> day nor night: ye that make mention of the Lord,
> keep not silence, 7 And give him no rest, till he
> establish, and till he make Jerusalem a praise in
> the earth.* Isaiah 62:6

God gave Isaiah strategy from an exiled Babylon. God
encouraged him through this scripture. There was a
prophetic word he was waiting to see manifest.
Watchmen watch and guard over the Word of the Lord.

They give the Word back to God until he releases His
promises in the earth realm. So, the position of the
watchman is to protect our destinies. They can see things
afar off. The titanic did not have the equipment to see
from afar what they hit. On the surface it just looked like
a small iceberg but under the water was massive ice that
caused the great damage that sunk, at that time, the
unsinkable.

Watchmen can see danger and block it with a Divine wall of protection, so that the enemy cannot infiltrate us. They have two assignments: they watch for the enemy and they discern where the enemy is hiding. They also watch for the moves of God and what He is releasing, work with gate keepers, and announce the move of God so the gate keepers know when to open the gates. Gate keepers represent leadership. Watchmen are influencers over nations, churches, and regions. Prophetic intercessors birth our destinies and Watchmen intercessors protect our destinies.

We see many churches' prophetic intercessors birthing destinies but no watchman intercessors to guard over and protect the destinies. Therefore, so many churches and businesses fail. All these administrations of prayer are vital.

Prayer warriors deal with the issues at hand or that are occurring but the Watchmen intercessors deal with what is a far off. Watchmen act ahead of the incident (time) and when you try to warn people, they think you are crazy because they do not understand you. I remember telling a pastor there was a witch in the ministry and then told him she would not stay long, but before she left, she would plant seeds of discord. I was told by him that I should just pray and not share everything with him. Well I was instructed by Holy Spirit to tell him. It was discarded and half the church left before the witch was prayed out of the ministry. Sometimes you will feel overwhelmed and alone as an intercessor but be encouraged God called you to it.

In a nutshell, intercessors are priestly, and they plead our cases before the throne of heaven, so heaven can intervene in the affairs of men. Prayer warriors are given prayer strategies and tactics, so we can receive breakthrough in our lives. Prophetic intercessors birth our destinies and read heaven's sonograms, to cause heaven to contract and release what is in the spirit realm. Watchmen build a divine wall of protection around us so the enemy cannot infiltrate territories.

Prayer

Father I pray supernatural over the readers natural, that you will impart the spirit of prayer over them.

Also, that they recognize their type in the spirit. Seek out the intercessors and call them to your throne of grace to do your will and walk out the purpose you have for them in the realm of the Spirit. Amen.

CHAPTER FOUR

Which Watch Are You?

*Therefore, confess your sins to each other and pray for
each other so that you may be healed. The prayer of a
righteous person is powerful and effective.*
James 5:16 (NIV)

Did you catch that? The "prayer of a righteous man is
powerful and effective." As we pray, we stand watch
over our families, cities, and nations. Just as men stood
on city walls in the Bible to watch for approaching
danger, God calls us to be modern-day watchmen and
warn those who are in danger (2 Kings 9:17-18). We are
to watch for the enemy's plot but also for the
manifestation of God's plans. If we watch for the enemy
and announce his activity, we can stop the devil's plans
to steal, kill and destroy what God has for us. Jesus said
in Matthew 24:43, *but know this, if the good man of the
house had known in what watch the thief would come, he
would have watched and would not have suffered his
house to be broken up.*

Now more than ever, it is important that we pray and
seek the mind of the Lord—as in Matthew 6:10, *thy
Kingdom come, Thy will be done in earth, as it is in
heaven.* Major decisions we are confronted with require
us to know God's individual Will for our lives. With
Holy Spirit's leading, we can discover God's Will and
expose the plans of the enemy through strategic prayer.

The Bible speaks of watches which are specific times of
the day or night. There are eight watches covering 24

hours. This is because everyone has a prayer watch, even though you may not know it. Therefore, you may find yourself repeatedly praying at specific times of the day or evening. If you have ever been awakened during the night or are wondering why you are being led to pray at specific times, it is probably because God wants you to pray or intercede for someone.

Every prayer watch has a purpose and understanding each watch will help you know the most strategic times to pray for God's will to be done in your life and in the lives of others.

Let us look at the eight prayer watches:

6 PM TO 9 PM

The first prayer watch begins in the evening, which is the <u>foundation of night</u>. The evening is a time for us to relax and be with family. It is also a time when we reflect upon what occurred during the day (good or bad) and pray a prayer of thanksgiving to God for being with us and bringing us through it.

> *And to stand every morning to thank and*
> *praise the Lord, and likewise at even:*
> 1 Chronicles 23:30

<u>Time for Meditation</u>

In addition to reflection and prayer, the first prayer watch is a time to meditate on God's Word. Meditation quiets our emotions, realigns our mind, and frees us to hear God speaking to us. What we could not hear clearly earlier in the day, we begin to hear during this time. During this watch, ask God to give you clear directions for the next day and insight into His call on your life!

<u>Time for Covenant Renewal with God</u>

God's covenant is found in the Bible and one of the many covenant benefits we have is healing. Jesus healed many sick and demon-possessed people during this time (Mark 1:32, Luke 4:40). This watch is usually for those who have a strong apostolic calling and anointing to break strongholds and walls. At this time, seasoned Christians are determined to do mighty things with boldness in the Lord.

If we begin to pray strategically during this watch with Holy Spirit's leading, we can prevent the kingdom of darkness from releasing curses on the new day.

WHAT YOU SHOULD BE PRAYING FOR DURING THIS TIME...

- Healing and deliverance through the resurrection power of Jesus.
- Covenant renewal with the Author and Finisher of your faith.
- Meditation and inner reflection to give thanks unto the Lord.
- Preparation as you await the arrival of dreams and visions in the night.
- Inquire about clarity for your day and concerning your ministry call.
- Pray for revelation and insight to dismantle destructive walls of darkness.
- Pronounce God's blessings upon your life, family, church, city, and the nation.

- Regroup your thoughts, and to be still and know that Jehovah is God.
- Release all anxiety to the Lord and purge yourself from the cares of the day.
- Shake and break down all the wicked structures from our economic systems, educational systems, religious systems, political systems, and all other systems.

Arise, cry out in the night: in the beginning of the watches pour out thine heart like water before the face of the Lord. Lamentations 2:19

The second prayer watch is the time in which intercessors can impact the spiritual realm before the enemy gets ready to carry out the plans and plots of evil. In the natural, this watch is characterized by deep darkness. In the spiritual realm, this is the time when diabolical assignments and sabotage from the enemy are set in motion. Have you ever noticed that during this time you hear police, ambulance, and fire truck sirens? Because this is the time people start to settle in for the night and the enemy starts to carry out his plans.

9PM TO 12AM

Pray for God's Intervention

During this watch, it is important for intercessors to pray for God's protection over their families, cities, and nations:

Let God arise, let his enemies be scattered: let them also that hate him flee before him. Psalm 68:1

The Bible tells us that midnight is a time when God intervenes and deals with the enemies that are trying to keep us from entering His perfect plan for our lives. Psalm 119:62 says, *at midnight I will rise to give thanks unto thee because of thy righteous judgments.*

According to Exodus 12:29-31, it was at the midnight hour that God struck down the first-born of Egypt, which resulted in His people being released from captivity and set free to worship Him.

This watch is a time for divine judgments, deliverance, prayer for the economy, tearing down walls of darkness and all the wicked structures from our economic, educational, religious, and political systems.

WHAT YOU SHOULD BE PRAYING FOR DURING THIS TIME...

- Worship and thanksgiving to acknowledge the Lord God Almighty.
- Blessing and divine favor as the outpouring of Father's love saturates your heart.
- Encounter and engagement to receive many acts of change in the earth.
- Break down, destroy, and demolish all demonic spirits sent on assignment.
- Operate in authority as strategies and keys are given to open and close doors.
- Pray for divine protection and provision to accomplish God's work.
- Pray that God arises, and His enemies are scattered, never to return!
- Time for prophetic utterance to command all creations to praise the Lord our God.

- Time to read and pray out loud, Psalm 148, Psalm 59, and Psalm 68:1-4.
- Time to see the Light of God as it shines to dismantle darkness in the midnight hour.

The third prayer watch is a period of much spiritual activity. This watch hour will strengthen your faith. It is the same time that Peter denied Christ three times. (Matthew 26:74, Mark 14:30, Luke 22:34, and John 13:38)

12AM TO 3AM

The Witching Hour

This watch is the darkest and most demonic part of the night, especially at midnight. Witches, warlocks, and satanists have fun and start their incantations during this part of the night. The devil operates during this time because this is the time that men are in a deep sleep and there are not as many people praying to oppose him. This watch calls for seasoned intercessors.

You must not be afraid of witchcraft during this watch. The Lord has given us dominion and authority over all things. This watch is geared for those who already know how to use their spiritual armor and war against the enemy. This is the time to pray against satanic attacks on your life, family members, marriages, churches, and communities. We are most vulnerable to the devil's attacks because during this time we are asleep. Declare Psalm 91:5-6 for Divine protection for yourself, family, church, city, and the nation.

WHAT YOU SHOULD BE PRAYING FOR DURING THIS TIME...

- Time of enlargement to explore new territories and possess new boundaries.
- Time of outpouring to overcome limitations blocking your gifts and talents.
- Time of spiritual breakthrough to achieve the plan and purpose for your life.
- Time to be alert and watchful as you receive wisdom, understanding, and insight.
- Time to war against plots, plans, and schemes of darkness and deception.
- Time to exercise dominion to possess the land flowing with milk and honey.
- Time to obtain clear direction to order your steps upon a lighted path.
- Time to pray and fortify yourself against worry, doubt, fear, and unbelief.
- Time to pray bold and aggressive prayers of protection and strength.
- Time to root out, pluck up, pull down and destroy all of Satan's devices.
- Time to shake foundations through the roar of your voice. *Hallelujah*!

3:00 AM. to 6:00 AM.

This fourth watch is always important because this is the last watch of the night. This watch is the time that the satanic agents who went out to perform their activities are returning to their bases.

Time for deliverance, to rise and shine, for resurrection

This is time for deliverance according to Exodus 12 and 14. This is also the time Jesus walked on the water to release the disciples from the storms (Matthew 14:25-33).

Command your morning

This is a disciplined prayer watch for those who have the power and training to wake up early in the morning and set the atmosphere. This prayer watch sets our day before it begins. This is an opportunity to set things in place before the devil and his demons have a chance to ruin it. Accidents, deaths, thefts, job losses, and any other acts of the devil can be stopped during this watch when intercessors obey the voice of the Lord and fill the morning with powerful prayers.

Time for Declaring God's Word

This is a time for angelic activity or intervention and a time for blessings from heaven. When we pray, the Lord hears our prayer and sends His angels to work on our behalf.

WHAT YOU SHOULD BE PRAYING FOR DURING THIS TIME...

- Time to ask the new day to speak into your life according to God's will (Psalm 19:2).
- Time for all the enemy's plans and strategies to fail.

- Pray for gaining territory, establishing the spirit of prosperity, and stopping the devil from hijacking blessings and favor.
- Consecrate all the work for the day and pray for protection for God's people throughout the day.

6:00 AM. - 9:00 AM.

This fifth watch is the time that God strengthens Christians (Acts 2: 15; Psalm 2:7-9). The spiritual significance of sunrise is having Jesus Christ, the King of Kings and the Lord of Lords, rise over us (Malachi 4:2).

Acts 2:15 says it was the "third hour of the day" (or 9:00 A.M.) when the Holy Spirit descended in the Upper Room on the day of Pentecost to equip the 120 disciples for service.

WHAT YOU SHOULD BE PRAYING FOR DURING THIS TIME...

- Pray for such issues as healing in your body, relationships, family, government, and the economy.
- Time to be equipped by the Holy Spirit for service (2 Corinthians 9:3; Ephesians 4:12)
- As you step out, ask God to equip you for the day.

9:00 A.M. to 12:00 P.M.

Time for a harvest of God's promises

In the sixth watch, the watchman guards, and watches for the Word of the Lord to be fulfilled.

Prayer for Provision to do God's Work (Exodus 11 :3-4)

This is the time to receive the supply of all resources needed for every God-given project (Exodus 12:35-36). It was the time that the Israelites got everything that they had to use to build the Tabernacle in the wilderness.

Jesus was crucified at the third hour, or 9:00 A.M. (Mark 15:25, Matthew 27:45). After having been on the cross for three hours, darkness came upon the face of the earth at 12:00 P.M. and continued until 3:00 P.M., when the period of darkness ended. Notice that even God worked according to the watches of the day, especially pertaining to the crucifixion events.

Prayer for a crucified life

It is generally accepted that this period marked both Christ's sentencing by Pilate and His crucifixion. This is the time to put off the old man and put on the Lord Jesus Christ (Colossians 3:2-11). This is the time to nail witchcraft, bitterness, jealousy, anger, backbiting, gossip, slander, lying, deception, hypocrisy and all the properties and personality traits of the devil and all the works of the flesh to the Cross (Galatians 2:20; 5:19-21).

"Forgive us for our trespasses ... as we forgive"

This is the best time to pray this portion of the model prayer the Lord Jesus Christ taught His disciples. The Israelites also observed this period as a time for corporate prayer. It was at this daily time of prayer and instruction at the Temple in Jerusalem that Peter and John were attending when they healed the lame man at the Gate Beautiful (Acts 2: 1-8).

WHAT YOU SHOULD BE PRAYING FOR DURING
THIS TIME...

- Time to see the manifestation of God's promises for your life as in the case of David in 2 Samuel 7:25-29.
- Pray for the provision to accomplish whatever God wants you to do.
- Time to appropriate the benefits of the Cross (healing, prosperity, forgiveness, strength, etc.).
- Ask God to help you manifest all the values of a crucified life, by mortifying the deeds of your flesh as stated in Romans 8: 12-15.
- Prayer for forgiveness, healing of relationships and the release of others.

12:00 P.M. to 3:00 P.M.

The seventh watch, midday, is an hour of rest and a time to seek the Lord. Historically, Christ was on the cross atoning for the sins of the world. Redemption and restoration for mankind manifests through God's Son. Peter received the vision of the clean and unclean animals which initiated the inclusion of the Gentiles in God's redemptive plan. Also, it was during this watch that Daniel always went home to pray.

Time of the Secret Place of the Most High (Psalm 91:1)

It is very important to pray in line with Acts 10:9 and Psalm 91:5-6, 14. This is the time to pray to "dwell in the secret place of the Most High, abiding under the shadow of the Almighty," and making the Most High your habitation. Pray and cut off all satanic arrows that are released at this time so that they will not get you or your family.

<u>Time of letting your light shine brighter until the full light of day is attained (Prov. 4:18)</u>

The midday is the beginning of the sixth hour (12:00 P.M.) This is the time when the sun is at its fullest and brightest.

WHAT YOU SHOULD BE PRAYING FOR DURING THIS TIME...

- Time to seek the Lord.
- Time that the promises of God are released, foundations are shaken, and to exercise your God-given dominion.
- Pray that your life would be bright.
- Pray not to be led into any temptation, trap, or snare of the enemy.

3:00 P.M. - 6:00 P.M.

The eighth watch is the hour of Revelation, hour of grace, hour of the voice of the Lord, and the hour of Triumph. This is the time to die to the world and to self.

<u>Time to Change or Shape History</u>

This was the time God changed history because this watch happens to be the time that Jesus died on the Cross (3:00 P.M). Jesus went through six hours of suffering for the deliverance of humankind and the world. When Jesus died, history was changed forever because He became our Blood Covenant with God and triumphed over hell, death, and the grave. Rejoice that you have turned your back on sin because you have been cleansed by the Blood of Jesus (1 John 1:7).

WHAT YOU SHOULD BE PRAYING FOR DURING THIS TIME...

- Pray for deliverance during this watch.
- Pray for power to have the same victory as Jesus did.
- Time to Remove anything that is limiting, as this is *The Hour of Power and Triumphant Glory!*

CHAPTER FIVE

Follow the Crumbs

Let us take a moment to see what it means to get what we need, by following God in prayer to a place of answered prayer. Faith is what leads us to the answers in God. I am sure you have asked the question *what do crumbs have to do with prayer?* The answer is everything. Just work with me on this one. First, we need to explore pursuing righteousness.

What does it mean to pursue righteousness?

Answer: Proverbs 15:9 says, *The LORD detests the way of the wicked, but he loves those who pursue righteousness.* If God wants us to pursue righteousness, then what about verses such as Romans 3:10 that says, *there is none righteous, no not one*? If no one is righteous, then who can really pursue it?

Before we can pursue righteousness, we need to define it. The word most often translated righteousness can also mean justice, justness, or divine holiness. It can also be defined as the condition of being acceptable to God as made possible by God. God's standard is what defines true righteousness; His power is what enables it. Unless God is its author, we will never possess righteousness. No amount of manmade effort will result in righteousness. To be righteous is to be right with God. A heart that is right with God results in a life that bears fruit (John 15:1–2; Mark 4:20). Galatians 5:22-23 lists some of that fruit.

A common substitute for true righteousness is self-righteousness. Self-righteousness is the opposite of what God desires. Our self-righteousness makes a list of rules and we check them off, patting ourselves on the back on how well our righteousness is doing compared to others. The Pharisees were masters of self-righteousness, but Jesus had hard words for them...

> *"Woe to you, teachers of the law and Pharisees, you hypocrites! You are like whitewashed tombs, which look beautiful on the outside but on the inside are full of the bones of the dead and everything unclean. 28 In the same way, on the outside you appear to people as righteous but on the inside you are full of hypocrisy and wickedness..."* (Matthew 23:27–28).

Wow imagine that being said to you. In the same way on the outside you appear to people as righteous but, on the inside, you are *"full of hypocrisy and wickedness."*

To pursue righteousness means we must acknowledge that we cannot please God in our sinful state (Romans 8:8). We must turn from trying to justify ourselves by our good works and instead seek after the mercy of God. We should desire that He transform our minds (Romans 12:2) and conform us to the image of His Son Jesus (Romans 8:29). In the Old Testament, men were declared righteous when they believed God and acted on it (Genesis 15:6; Galatians 3:6; James 2:23). Before Pentecost (Acts 2:1–4), people pursued righteousness by keeping God's Law, seeking holiness, and walking humbly with God (Micah 6:8). No one was justified by rule keeping but by the faith that enabled them to obey God (Romans 3:20; Galatians 2:16).

Even today we are justified by the faith that leads us to Jesus (Romans 3:28; 5:1; 10:10). Those who are in Christ continue seeking God to please Him (Colossians 3:1). When we come to faith in Christ, He gives us Holy Spirit who empowers us to pursue righteousness for its own sake (Acts 2:38). He commands us to walk in the Spirit (Galatians 5:16, 25). Walking in the Spirit means we live a lifestyle of total surrender to the Lordship of Jesus Christ. We cultivate the ability to hear God and the habit of obeying His voice in everything.

We pursue righteousness when we pursue the character of Christ and desire holiness more than fleshly indulgence. We avoid the temptation to become self-righteous when we understand that true righteousness begins with Godly humility (Psalm 25:90). We remember that Jesus said ...*apart from me you can do nothing* (John 15:5). When we spend time in the presence of God, we become more aware of our own sin and shortcomings. A dirty shirt looks white beside a dark wall. But when compared with snow, the same shirt looks dirty. Pride and self-righteousness cannot remain in the presence of a Holy God. Pursuing righteousness begins when a humble heart seeks the continual presence of God (James 4:10; 1 Peter 5:6). The humble, believing heart leads to a lifestyle of righteous action acceptable to God (Psalm 51:10).

So now let us talk about the CRUMBS in Matthew 15:21-28; there was a mother a Canaanite woman who was a gentile. She desperately wanted her daughter to be healed and delivered from a demon that possessed her. Like so many parents desiring a breakthrough for their children. You may be a parent that has been praying for your child to be delivered or healed. She sought after

Jesus (righteousness) for the sake of her child. You can read the story; I want to just point out the main things as we can relate it to prayer.

This woman was not considered to be a believer or accepted as one of God's own. She pursued Jesus because she was aware of His ability and reputation to heal her daughter. She did not care if she had a right to what everyone else had as God's chosen. When you get to the place of desperation, you will humble yourself and chase after righteousness because you know justice is wrapped in it. She spoke her petition that her daughter was possessed and needed healing. Jesus ignored her at first but that did not stop her. How many times have you gone to God and felt like He was ignoring you in prayer? She did not give up because her love and tenacity for her daughter's life caused her to be humble. She was a woman of faith, yet she was not even considered a Jew. She was chasing the righteous one on behalf of her sick child. In Mark 2:17 Jesus said, *He came not for the righteous but the sinners and those who are sick.* Now that alone should boost your prayer life for healing of unsaved and sick loved ones.

Let us look at the conversation between the woman and Jesus. Again, you must go read the story for yourself. After ignoring her she continued until Jesus addressed her with this response for her request to heal her daughter. He said in verse 25-28; I will paraphrase it. He said, is it right to take the children's bread and toss it to the dogs? She did not speak out of hurt nor did she ask, "DID JESUS JUST CALL ME A DOG?"

No, she humbled herself before the Great Intercessor. She responded, "Yes, it is, Lord" (she recognized who

He was). She went on to say, "Even the dogs eat the crumbs from the master's table." Listen if Jesus wants to call me a dog then He can go ahead; I am desperate for a breakthrough. Humility and faith in prayer will get God's attention any day. Then Jesus said to her, "Woman you have great faith! YOUR REQUEST IS GRANTED." Her daughter was healed that moment.

Your prayer life is hinged on your righteousness, humility, and faith. He showed mercy towards her because she postured herself in humility and he recognized her faith in her request. We are to go boldly to the throne of grace believing God will reward us. He rewarded her. So, to answer your question, why call this chapter CRUMBS? The woman was willing to take the crumbs because what is in the crumbs is in the bread He spoke of. She Chased Righteousness Until Miracles and Blessings Showed up. There you have C.R.U.M.B.S. No matter how small or big your request, He is no respecter of persons. You can have the same outcome because He is righteous like that.

CHAPTER SIX

<u>Destiny Has an Appointment</u>

Definition of appointment:

an arrangement to meet someone at a time and place.

What is the relationship between God and time?

The Bible describes God's relationship to time in several places. Psalm 90:4 says, *for a thousand years in your sight are but as yesterday when it is past, or as a watch in the night.* Second Peter 3:8 says, *with the Lord one day is as a thousand years, and a thousand years as one day.* Isaiah 57:15 says that God *inhabits eternity.*

When we say things like God is timeless or God has no beginning or end, we are trying to explain God in terms of a dimension by which He is not constrained. God created time.

In the universe time is basically progressing from one stage to another in a single series of steps, time is sequential. We go forward at a steady rate. We cannot go back in time, and we cannot experience more than one instant at a time.

God does not have this limitation. He does not live within the timeline of our universe. He experiences every moment of time all at once. Imagine that if you can understand this, you will have a better understanding of God's power in our lives. He was able to create the world in six days because days do not confine Him or His work

(Genesis 1). He was able to choose who to save before the days and years began (2 Timothy 1:9) because He created them. And He is able to select good works for us to do ahead of time (Ephesians 2:10) because He can see everything that will ever happen in human history and exactly how we can be the most effective to use that history to bring people to Him. When He says He has a plan for us (Jeremiah 29:11) that plan is based on His perfect knowledge of all of history, present, and future. When we do not trust His plan, it is the ultimate foolishness like ignoring the advice of a perfect GPS because we think we know a better route.

God's timelessness is part of His perfection. He has no need of growth or development or any of the other benefits time gives us. He also has no temporal beginning or end. He has neither our need for time neither our time related limitations, which is just another example of why we can trust Him with our short temporal lives.

When you pray do you expect God to answer as soon as you rise from your knees? I used to be that way. But learning to have patience has taught me how to wait on the timing of God; although, there is an appointed time. We must trust that appointed time. Not trusting God creates our inability to wait.

He promised Sarah and Abraham a child and they could not wait because of their age and or just got tired of waiting. They tried to do what God already did but not manifested. They had Abraham sleep with the maidservant and Ishmael was born. Because of this a war is going on now between the two seeds fighting for a birth right. When we do not allow the appointed time for our destinies, we cause major problems.

Imagine Jesus doing what He wanted and not going to the cross. Where would we be? I shake to think. Let us go to the garden of gethsemane. We go before God to take away or to give, but what are we wanting Him to give us and to take away? Most times we want Him to take away what hurt us when in fact, what hurt sometimes is what He prescribes and is part of our destiny. Philippians 4:6 states, *do not be anxious about anything, but in every situation, by prayer and petition, with thanksgiving, present your requests to God.* If Jesus who was on His way to destiny (THE CROSS) can go before God and pray, who are we to not keep our destinies on schedule with prayer.

Prayer will save you pain, time, money and even your life. Jesus took three close disciples with Him when He went to pray. He wanted them to learn, also to be watchmen over His destiny in prayer. Even Jesus desired reinforcement if I can say that. He agonized in going through His process to be the sacrifice to save a world that refused Him. Yet, He prayed because He knew the appointed time to go to the cross was near. He needed prayer to keep Him on the time, set before the foundation of the earth. You do not think He saw what Eve did in the garden? He knew then He would have to die a brutal death. I do not think He was in heaven telling the Father I am not dying for them, seeing all He would endure before anyone of the accusers were even born. That is a real Destiny Shaker—the ultimate Destiny Shaker.

We must allow ourselves to be pruned and disciplined in prayer to the point of understanding the timing of God.

His time is so perfect. I would never have written this book if I did not understand the timing of God. With you reading this now is part of your destiny. Nothing we do is wasted or by chance. My prayer for you while reading this chapter is that you understand how important your life is to God that you wait on Him for everything.

All you have done and will do good, bad, or ugly has been part of the path to your destiny. If you do not know what that is, then go to your garden of Gethsemane and seek God for your cup. We all have one and asking for it to pass you is not the question. God will send angels like He sent to Jesus to strengthen you. Take up your cross today and walk it out. Your Destiny has an appointment and prayer keeps it on schedule.

CHAPTER SEVEN

A Place Called the Altar

An Altar is a structure on which offerings are made to a deity. The Hebrew word for altar is mizbeah from a verbal root meaning "to slaughter." Greek renders this word as "a place of sacrifice." An altar is a place where sacrifice is offered.

Altars could be natural objects or manmade constructs. Four materials are recorded as being used in altars: stone, earth, metal, and brick. Archaeology has provided numerous examples of altars from Palestine dating back to approximately 3000 b.c. Natural rocks were also used (Judges 6:20). An altar could stand alone.

Altars were places where the divine and human worlds interacted. Altars were places of exchange, communication, and influence. God responded actively to altar activity. The contest between Elijah and the prophets of Baal involving an altar demonstrated interaction between God and Baal. Noah built an altar and offered a sacrifice to God. God smelled the aroma and found it pleasing. He responded to Noah's action by declaring that he would never again destroy all living things through a flood. In the patriarchal period, altars were markers of place, commemorating an encounter with God (Gen 12:7), or physical signs of habitation. Abraham built an altar where he pitched his tent between Bethel and Ai.

Presumably at that altar he *called on the name of the Lord* (Gen 12:8). Interestingly, we are not told if there was a response. In the next passage, however, Abraham went to Egypt and fell into sin, lying about Sarah out of fear of Pharaoh. Perhaps there was no true communication at the altar between Bethel and Ai.

When it comes to prayer, we should have an altar on our heart. One that is dedicated to God, an altar of the days of old were physical places where the patriarchs met God and named the place of the encounters. They also offered up animal sacrifices. We no longer must do that, but the altars can still be a place, posture, or principle. The first time an altar was mentioned in the bible was to set precedence.

That is what is called the law of first mention. It set the standard. In the new testament Romans 12:1 (NIV) says, *Therefore, I urge you, brothers and sisters, in view of God's mercy, to offer your bodies as a living sacrifice, holy and pleasing to God—this is your true and proper worship.* An altar is a place of worship, offering, thanksgiving, surrender, healing, and deliverance. The place called altar is where God makes covenants (promises), reveals Himself or is used for (Revelation), Worship (to meet God) and a place of prayer.

In 1Samuel 1:9-20, Hannah prayed before God on the altar for a child and God made her a promise on that altar. The altar is also a place of faith. God promised Abraham land to his descendants and I like to believe at that place was the beginning of Abraham's faith. He would later come back to that place and was reminded of that promise. What have you set as a place to meet God? Every Destiny Shaker in the bible had a place they met with God. When God asked Solomon what he wanted and would have given him whatever he wanted, Solomon asked for wisdom and God granted it. Solomon built an altar to God, offered a sacrifice, and prayed. After he prayed, fire came down on the altar. That was God showing that He was pleased with the altar and the offering.

God wants to light fire on your altar of prayer and sacrifice. We can set a place in our home where we meet God. Where have you met God and experienced His presence? Is it a favorite chair you pray in, a closet you go in, is it the edge of your bed, your dining room or kitchen table? No matter the place when you create space and time for God He will show up. It is your worship and sacrifice He is after, that is the sweet smell He is looking for.

Even during an altar call in your church, the sanctuary should be respected. When salvation is being offered to people even in their seats, that becomes an altar as soon as they decide to surrender all to God. It really bothers me when people start to move in the sanctuary when salvation is offered, it disturbs the atmosphere and the person that has made that moment of worship an altar moment with God. We should respect the sacred things of God as Noah already set precedence for the altar. The law of first mention is not void of the principle of the altar.

Take this time to think of a place, posture, and principle of your altar. This may be the moment and right where you are now God is meeting you. This is your place called the Altar.

CHAPTER EIGHT

Court Is in Session

The court of heaven is the realm of God where legal proceedings take place. Everything done in the universe both spiritual and physical has a legal backing from the Court. Like every legal system, there are different types of courts.

My engaging the court on a personal level and intercession has opened my eyes to a different world of possibility in God. I will not go into doctrine or extensive teaching knowing it has been done by respected leaders. Get materials from Robert Henderson who has amazing teachings in his series of books.

Just as in the natural there are different courts in heaven. In the natural you must have a case with a legal issue to approach the judge. There is the magistrate, civil, criminal, and preliminary hearings for more serious cases. You have the judge or a civil officer in the court of law. Either you present a case, or one is brought up against you and there must be a legal reason to do so. Now let us look at this situation where a case was brought up before God. In Job 1:6-7, this is a clear case the devil brought up before God. He wanted to put Job's faith on trial; his dedication to God was also on trial.

> *One day the angels came to present themselves before the LORD, and Satan also came with them. 7 The LORD said to Satan, "Where have you come from?" Satan answered the LORD, "From roaming throughout the earth, going*

*back and forth on it." 8Then the LORD said to
Satan, "Have you considered my servant Job?
There is no one on earth like him; he is
blameless and upright, a man who fears God
and shuns evil." 9" Does Job fear God for
nothing?" Satan replied. 10" Have you not put
a hedge around him and his household and
everything he has? You have blessed the work of
his hands, so that his flocks and herds are
spread throughout the land. 11But now stretch
out your hand and strike everything he has, and
he will surely curse you to your face." 12The
LORD said to Satan, "Very well, then,
everything he has is in your power, but on the
man himself do not lay a finger." Then Satan
went out from the presence of the LORD.*
Job 1:6-12

The enemy is looking to see whom he can devour, He
walks back and forth waiting on you and or your seed to
do something to gain legal access to take your right for
the promises of God from you. The place to fight in
prayer for your bloodline is in the court of heaven. As I
mentioned before I remember My sister was facing years
in prison for being associated with someone who was
doing illegal activities. She was facing 30 years. I was in
prayer for her and I heard God say go on a 40 day fast.

During the fast I was instructed to stay home the day she
went to court and pray during the time she was in court.
I was obedient and I prayed during the time. No one was
allowed in the court at the time but the defendants, DA,
and defense attorney. Long story short, while I was in
prayer, I was able to see in the spirit everything that was
going on. It was as if I was sitting in the room. God gave

me the words to pray and I moved in the spirit in that room. When it was all over and done my sister walked away from everything the enemy tried to use to snare her. OUT of everyone in that case she was the only one that was exonerated and did not go to jail. You cannot tell me that God is not a judge on the throne for us.

The enemy only has legal access to you when you give it to him. Job was found not guilty in the case against his faith in God. No matter what he lost he never gave up on God and God had everything needed to rule in his favor. Again, I will not try to teach the court in heaven in this book. I just know that what is done in the natural is also done in the spirit. I offer a 12-week course through the prayer clinic and more teaching can be done there.

You must know that everything stolen from you is restored in the court of heaven. Satan tried Jesus in the wilderness, He wanted Jesus to give him legal rights to the throne, but Jesus fought back with the legalities of the WORD OF GOD. Satan had to flee because Jesus knew He already had what satan was offering Him. To be honest, satan was offering Jesus what Adam and Eve gave him and Jesus came to take it back on the cross. The devil is so stupid. Do not be stupid and give him what Jesus gave back to you. When you get in prayer tell him Court is in session and watch him shake from fear of you—Them Destiny Shakers!

CHAPTER NINE

Prayer Changes Things

We are blessed to have a Father in heaven that we can always approach with confidence, especially when we need a miracle or blessing. It is important to remember that God has not forgotten or abandoned us. The word of God tells us, *the LORD Himself goes before you and will be with you; He will never leave you nor forsake you. Do not be afraid; do not be discouraged* (Deuteronomy 31:8). God has also promised to answer every prayer according to His amazing grace, His infinite powerful authority, and in keeping with His infinite love and faithfulness. Our attitude should be one of unshakable confidence that He is able to do exceedingly more than all we ask or imagine, according to His power that is working within us. Often, we neglect to ask God for miracles in our lives and end up settling for less than God's best for us. The truth is, we can always approach God with confidence if we trust in His Son, Jesus Christ. We also know that prayer has incredible power to change things.

What does prayer change?

Prayer stopped the plans of Haman who wanted to kill the people of God because Esther prayed. It stopped Lot and his family from dying in Sodom because Abraham prayed for him. I can name several stories of how prayer changed situations, but you know the stories. Prayer is very powerful. It is a weapon and it is protection. I remember when growing up my grandmothers would pray for us. Whenever we would say we wanted to go to a park, school dance or skating my grandmother would cover us. One specific thing I do remember. Wherever we said we were going, she would ask that we be covered on that journey, at our destination, and on the journey back home. As I grew in the things of God, I understood why. The protection would go where we said we were going.

If we went somewhere other than where we said something would happen. I believe that was because the protection was for where we said we were going. Do not get me wrong, God is sovereign, and He can go wherever He desires. However, when we are in rebellion we are in sin and He can step back and let us learn from disobedience; too bad I did not learn that earlier. So as a parent I made sure and still make sure that my prayers of protection go everywhere with them—places I am aware of and even when they step out of where they should be. Prayer changes us from the inside out.

Your faith life corresponds directly to the quality of your prayer life. Prayer has the power to change the people and things around you. Prayer also has the power to change you on the inside and outside. When you need strength, remember that God is the healer and can guide you in endless ways. If your heart and life are centered on God, His Word, and Holy Spirit, you can be assured that He will direct your path. Prayer builds your faith and it helps you to become closer to God. My time in prayer revealed to me the character and attributes of God. My struggles pushed me deeper into prayer and it revealed to me Him as a Father, a Healer and Provider and a Protector. During one of the hardest times I found a new place in prayer.

It changed my heart of bitterness towards my ex-husband. A man who publicly showed love and adoration towards me became someone I did not recognize immediately after marrying him. After four short months of getting married he left me and my daughter. I came home to an empty home with just mattresses on the floor and an eviction notice on the door. I found myself in the face of God seeking Him for a life changing miracle.

For 17 months I struggled to find my way back into living again. God revealed Himself to me in ways I had never seen before. I found my heavenly Father, Healer, Provider, Protector, and Defender. Prayer will restore everything lost. In prayer as a Destiny Shaker you must learn to listen, build patience, and surrender in God. You cannot shake the earth without a prayer life that does not change anything. It starts in us first. You have the power to change the world in prayer.

CHAPTER TEN

Destiny Shaker

Destiny shakers are people who do the things that others dream of doing, without fear or compromise. Your destiny is a series of events that will happen to shape your future. You are a conduit used by God for the shaking in the earth.

They do not just rock the boat and make waves; they are involved in what God is doing in the world. As a result, they find themselves in the company of other destiny shakers. Destiny Shakers are those who hear the voice of God. They release revelation to those who are positioned to receive it. You must not only have a personal relationship with Jesus, but also walk in awareness of His presence, have an expectation to hear His voice, and a prayer life that touches heaven.

God can speak through anything, and at any time. He will train you how to discern His voice from your own thoughts, motives, and intentions. A shaker must have an ear to hear God. They are intercessors, prophets, teachers, apostles, bishops, pastors, and evangelists. They have been processed through hell's fire all to the glory of God. They are determined by any means necessary that they will fulfill the plans and the will of God. Destiny Shakers go through so much, yet for God they live and for God they will die. The disciples were the first group of Destiny Shakers that walked with Jesus. They were taught to preach the gospel in the face of death. John the Baptist was a Destiny Shaker he prepared the way for the Messiah.

God will use the most unlikely to be Destiny Shakers. Moses was a murderer; God used him to deliver His people. Rahab was a prostitute who assisted the spies from being captured and she found herself right in the middle of the bloodline of Jesus. God used an orphaned girl Esther to save a nation through fasting and prayer. God used a widow woman Anna to cover the prophecy of the coming Messiah in prayer.

Hannah prayed and birthed the prophet Samuel. When we look at the lives of these shakers, we cannot help but think if God can use them with their flaws and backgrounds, can He use me? Yes, he can use you as well.

There are times I look at my own life and wonder why God wants to use me. I have been married and divorced four times. I have had extra marital affairs; yes, with an "s." I lived a very promiscuous life as a young woman. I was an alcoholic, a liar a shoplifter and a thief AKA booster. Oh, I have done my share of dirty deeds. But when I gave my heart to God, I gave Him the entire heart. Looking back over my life there have been dire situations in which I could have died, but He had a plan and even in my self-destructive ways, He would not let me die. He kept me for a time such as this. I embraced the yes, I gave Him, and will do whatever He asks of me. Looking at what Jesus did for me I could never set my heart to ever say no.

What has God delivered you from? What has He asked you to do that you feel you are not worthy of doing? We are not the judge of or the tour guide into our destiny. Everything you lived through has given you power and authority to shake someone loose from and out of the same mess. Jesus is the great intercessor and the Ultimate Destiny Shaker. God wants to shake the earth with His power, and He needs us to work through. When Jesus died on the cross for us, He shook the earth and all of hell. He shook the graves and the gates of hell to release the dead and captives.

Who were some of the Destiny Shakers of the old testament? Noah was laughed at for building the ark. His obedience saved his family and animals for God to replenish the earth after the flood. The ministry of Jesus shook lives. He met a woman at the well that was ashamed to gather with other women when it was all said and done, he made her an evangelist. He came to the aid of a woman who was caught in the act of adultery and told her to go sin no more. She became part of the great scriptures to be an example of the mercy and grace we all walk in.

The woman with the issue of blood was a Destiny Shaker. What made her one? She pushed past the crowd to take her own life back after trusting it in the hands of many physicians. You see the crowd she pushed through were men, the very ones who deemed her unclean. Whenever you take your life back out of the hand of the enemy you become a Destiny Shaker. That is powerful when you can do that. These are just examples to show you that God uses ordinary people and situations to shake and shape the world we live in, although these are people of the old testament.

Today they still have a great impact on our destiny. Nothing is new under the sun. Just different times, faces, names and the unnamed. But, the one Destiny Shaker that has a name above every name is Jesus the Great

Intercessor. The earth shaker and your Destiny Shaker. Let me leave you with this.

There will never be a question as to who the real Destiny Shaker is. JESUS! The one who was beaten beyond recognition, spit upon, hung, and stripped naked for all to see. The one who hung on a cross for hours in pain that cannot be described, hung between two thieves, and was treated horribly. The one who could barely breathe and was branded as a criminal, being innocent of everything of which He was accused. The one who had healed and delivered so many with proof of undeniable miracles. Being watched by a loving mother as He hung on the Roman cross of crucifixion. Yes, that was the one who thought God forgot and left Him. JESUS!

> *45 From noon until three in the afternoon darkness came over all the land. 46About three in the afternoon Jesus cried out in a loud voice, "Eli, Eli, lema sabachthani?" (which means "My God, my God, why have you forsaken me?"). 47When some of those standing there heard this, they said, "He's calling Elijah." 48Immediately one of them ran and got a sponge. He filled it with wine vinegar, put it on a staff, and offered it to Jesus to drink. 49The rest said, "Now leave him alone. Let us see if Elijah comes to save him." 50And when Jesus had cried out again in a loud voice, he gave up his spirit. 51At that moment the curtain of the temple was torn in two from top to bottom. The earth shook, the rocks split 52and the tombs broke open. The bodies of many holy people who had died were raised to life. 53They came out of the tombs after Jesus' resurrection and*

went into the holy city and appeared to many people. 54When the centurion and those with him who were guarding Jesus saw the earthquake and all that had happened, they were terrified, and exclaimed, "Surely he was the Son of God!" Matthew 27:45-54

WHAT IS HIS NAME? The Word. Jesus of Nazareth. Lamb of God. Messiah. The Way, the Truth, and the Life. Good Shepherd. Light of the World. King of kings. Prince of Peace. Son of God.

THE DESTINY SHAKER, THE ONE WHO LIVES IN YOU AND WHO MAKES YOU A DESTINY SHAKER!

Minister Carla Gaskins

Carla Gaskins is an inspirational, motivational speaker, author, the founder of Tamar's Heart Ministry, host of The Women Who Worship Conference and president of Life and Vision Connect Coaching, LLC—a personal and professional life coaching business. Carla empowers people to embrace purpose and life no matter the obstacles by promoting change, developing growth, and creating exceptional results through life coaching, innovative workshops, and Conferences, with the use of effective coaching models. Her coaching skills and life application strategies impacts lives and compels the leader within to strive for next level living.

As a sought-after conference speaker, mentor and workshop facilitator for churches, women's groups, and nonprofit organizations, she is known as the female architect, helping women rebuild their lives after divorce and tragedy. She was nominated for the Coalition for Women in Ministry Organization 2016 Esther award for her service to community and the local church. The annually anticipated conference, Women Who Worship draws women from around the country.

CPSIA information can be obtained
at www.ICGtesting.com
Printed in the USA
LVHW081111030322
712479LV00007B/230

9 781941 574171